THE GOLDEN WORLD OF
NURSERY RHYMES

SELECTED BY
JANE WERNER

ILLUSTRATED BY
ALICE AND MARTIN PROVENSEN

Galley Press

CONTENTS

OLD MOTHER GOOSE

Old Mother Goose, when
  She wanted to wander,
Would ride through the air
  On a very fine gander.

Mother Goose had a house,
  'Twas built in the wood,
Where an owl at the door
  For sentinel stood.

This is her son Jack,
  A plain-looking lad;
He is not very good,
  Nor yet very bad.

She sent him to market,
  A live goose he bought.
"Here, mother," says he.
  "It will not go for naught."

9

Jack's goose and her gander
    Grew very fond;
They'd both eat together,
    Or swim in one pond.

Jack found one fine morning,
    As I have been told,
His goose had laid him
    An egg of pure gold.

Jack rode to his mother,
    The news for to tell;
She called him a good boy
    And said it was well.

Jack sold his gold egg
    To a rascally knave;
Not half of its value
    To poor Jack he gave.

Then Jack went a-courting
    A lady so gay,
As fair as the lily,
    And sweet as the May.

The knave and the squire
    Came up at his back,
And began to belabor
    The sides of poor Jack.

And then the gold egg
    Was thrown into the sea,
When Jack he jumped in,
    And got it back presently.

The knave got the goose,
    Which he vowed he would kill,
Resolving at once
    His pockets to fill.

Jack's mother came in
    And caught the goose soon,
And, mounting its back,
    Flew up to the moon.

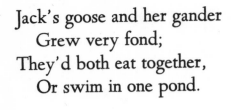

10

Cock Robin and Jenny Wren

'Twas on a merry time, when Jenny Wren was young,
So daintily she danced and so prettily she sung,
Robin Redbreast lost his heart, for he was a gallant bird,
So he doffed his hat to Jenny Wren, requesting to be heard.

"Oh, dearest Jenny Wren, if you will be but mine,
You shall feed on cherry pie and drink new currant wine.
I'll dress you like a goldfinch or any peacock gay,
So dearest Jen, if you'll be mine, let us appoint the day."

Jenny blushed behind her fan and thus declared her mind:
"Since, dearest Bob, I love you well, I'll take your offer kind.
Cherry pie is very nice and so is currant wine,
But I must wear my russet gown and never dress too fine."

Robin rose up early, before the break of day;
He flew to Jenny Wren's house, to sing a roundelay.
He met the cock and hen, and bade the cock declare,
This was his wedding day, with Jenny Wren the fair.

PEASE PORRIDGE HOT

Pease porridge hot,
Pease porridge cold,
Pease porridge in the pot,
Nine days old.

Some like it hot,
Some like it cold,
Some like it in the pot,
Nine days old.

Birds of a feather

Birds of a feather flock together,
    And so will pigs and swine;
Rats and mice will have their choice,
    And so will I have mine.

UP STREET, DOWN STREET

Up street, down street,
Each window's made of glass;
If you'll go to Tommy's house,
You'll find a pretty lass.

ROBIN-A-BOBBIN

Robin-a-Bobbin
Bent his bow,
Shot at a pigeon,
And killed a crow.

For every evil

For every evil under the sun
There is a remedy or there is none.
If there is one, seek till you find it;
If there be none, never mind it.

MAID MARIAN

Maid Marian is Queen of May,
All good children own her sway;
Her waist is white, her skirt is red,
A crown of gold is on her head.

On Christmas Eve

On Christmas Eve I turned the spit;
I burnt my fingers, I feel it yet;
The cock sparrow flew over the table,
The pot began to play with the ladle;
The ladle stood up like an angry man,
And vowed he'd fight the frying pan;
The frying pan behind the door
Said he never saw the like before;
And the kitchen clock I was going to wind,
Said he never saw the like behind.

A NICK AND A NOCK

A nick and a nock,
A hen and a cock,
And a penny for my master.

GREEN CHEESE

Green cheese, yellow laces,
Up and down the market places;
Turn, cheeses, turn.

TWO MONKEYS

Two monkeys came from native wood,
To view the haunts and ways of men;
Two mortal hours they silent stood,
And then, content, went back again.

FIDDLE-DE-DEE

Fiddle-de-dee, fiddle-de-dee,
The fly shall marry the bumblebee.
They went to church, and married was she;
The fly has married the bumblebee.

LITTLE BOY BLUE

Little Boy Blue, come blow your horn!
The sheep's in the meadow, the cow's in the corn.
Where's the boy that looks after the sheep?
He's under the haycock, fast asleep.
Will you wake him? No, not I;
For if I do, he'll be sure to cry.

A Frog He Would a-Wooing Go

"Now pray, Mr. Rat, won't you come with me?"
Heigho! says Rowley.
"Kind Mrs. Mousey for to see?"
With a rowley, powley, gammon and spinach,
Heigho! says Anthony Rowley.

And when they came to Mousey's hall,
Heigho! says Rowley.
They gave a knock and they gave a call,
With a rowley, powley, gammon and spinach,
Heigho! says Anthony Rowley.

A frog, he would a-wooing go,
Heigho! says Rowley.
Whether his mother would let him or no,
With a rowley, powley, gammon and spinach,
Heigho! says Anthony Rowley.

So off he set with his opera hat,
Heigho! says Rowley.
And on the way he met with a rat,
With a rowley, powley, gammon and spinach,
Heigho! says Anthony Rowley.

"Pray, Mrs. Mouse, are you within?"
Heigho! says Rowley.
"Yes, kind sirs, I'm sitting to spin."
With a rowley, powley, gammon and spinach,
Heigho! says Anthony Rowley.

"Pray, Mr. Frog, will you give us a song?"
Heigho! says Rowley.
"But let it be something that's not very long."
With a rowley, powley, gammon and spinach,
Heigho! says Anthony Rowley.

"Indeed, Mrs. Mouse, I shall have to say no."
Heigho! says Rowley.
"A cold has made me as hoarse as a crow."
With a rowley, powley, gammon and spinach,
Heigho! says Anthony Rowley.

"Since you have caught cold, Mr. Frog," Mousey said,
Heigho! says Rowley.
"I'll give you a song that I have just made."
With a rowley, powley, gammon and spinach,
Heigho! says Anthony Rowley.

Now while they all were merry-making,
Heigho! says Rowley.
A cat and her kittens came tumbling in,
With a rowley, powley, gammon and spinach,
Heigho! says Anthony Rowley.

As Froggy was crossing over a brook,
Heigho! says Rowley.
A lily-white duck came and gobbled him up,
With a rowley, powley, gammon and spinach,
Heigho! says Anthony Rowley.

So here is an end of one, two, three--
Heigho! says Rowley.
The Rat, and the Mouse and the little Frog-gee,
With a rowley, powley, gammon and spinach,
Heigho! says Anthony Rowley.

The cat, she seized the rat by the crown,
Heigho! says Rowley.
And the kittens pulled the little mouse down,
With a rowley, powley, gammon and spinach,
Heigho! says Anthony Rowley.

This put Mr. Frog in a terrible fright,
Heigho! says Rowley.
He put on his hat, and he wished them good night,
With a rowley, powley, gammon and spinach,
Heigho! says Anthony Rowley.

I Saw Three Ships

I saw three ships come sailing by,
Come sailing by, come sailing by,
I saw three ships come sailing by,
On New Year's Day in the morning.

And what do you think was in them then?
Was in them then, was in them then?
And what do you think was in them then,
On New Year's Day in the morning?

CROSS PATCH

Cross Patch,
Draw the latch,
Sit by the fire and spin;
Take a cup
And drink it up,
And call your neighbors in.

HERE SITS THE LORD MAYOR

Here sits the Lord Mayor,
   (point to forehead)
Here sit his two men,
   (eyes)
Here sits the cock,
   (cheek)
Here sits the hen,
   (other cheek)
Here sit the little chickens,
   (tip of nose)
Here they run in,
   (mouth)
Chin-chopper, chin-chopper,
   (chin)
   chin-chopper, chin!

LITTLE NANNY ETTICOAT
(A Riddle)

Little Nanny Etticoat
In a white petticoat
And a red nose;
The longer she stands
The shorter she grows.
   (A candle.)

ONE, TWO, THREE

One, two, three,
I love coffee,
And Billy loves tea.
How good you be!
One, two, three,
I love coffee,
And Billy loves tea.

KITTY THE SPINNER

Kitty the spinner
Will sit down to dinner,
And eat the leg of a frog.

All good people,
Look over the steeple,
And see the cat play with the dog.

Rub-a-Dub-Dub

Rub-a-dub-dub,
Three men in a tub;
And who do you think they be?
The butcher, the baker,
The candlestick-maker;
Turn 'em out, knaves all three!

HICKORY DICKORY

Hickory, dickory, dock!
The mouse ran up the clock;
The clock struck one,
And down he run,
Hickory, dickory, dock.

16

Come Sailing By

Three pretty girls were in them then,
Were in them then, were in them then,
Three pretty girls were in them then,
On New Year's Day in the morning.

And one could whistle, and one could sing,
And one could play on the violin;
Such joy there was at my wedding,
On New Year's Day in the morning.

DIBBITY, DIBBITY

Dibbity, dibbity, dibbity, doe,
  Give me a pancake
And I'll go.

Dibbity, dibbity, dibbity, ditter,
  Please to give me
A bit of a fritter.

Little Betty Blue

Little Betty Blue
Lost her holiday shoe;
What can little Betty do?
Give her another
To match the other
And then she may walk in two.

DAYS OF THE WEEK

Monday alone,
Tuesday together,
Wednesday we walk
When it's fine weather,
Thursday we kiss,
Friday we cry,
Saturday's hours
Seem almost to fly.
But of all the days
Of the week we will call
Sunday, the rest day,
The best day of all.

MR. PUNCHINELLO

Oh, Mother, I shall be married
To Mr. Punchinello,
To Mr. Punch,
To Mr. Joe,
To Mr. Nell,
To Mr. Low,
To Mr. Punch, Mr. Joe,
Mr. Nell, Mr. Low,
Mr. Punchinello.

BROW BRINKY

Brow brinky,
Eye winky,
Chin choppy,
Cheek, cherry,
Mouth merry.

IN FIR TAR IS

In fir tar is,
In oak none is.
In mud eel is,
In clay none is.
Goat eat ivy.
Mare eat oats.

THERE WAS A MAID

There was a maid on Scrabble Hill,
And if not dead, she lives there still;
She grew so tall, she reached the sky,
And on the moon, hung clothes to dry.

17

EVERY LADY IN THE LAND

Every lady in the land
Has twenty nails, upon each hand
Five, and twenty on hands and feet.
All this is true without deceit.

HOGS IN THE GARDEN

Hogs in the garden, catch 'em, Towser;
Cows in the corn-field, run, boys, run;
Cats in the cream-pot, run, girls, run;
Fire on the mountains, run, boys, run.

GOOSEY, GOOSEY, GANDER

Goosey, goosey, gander,
Whither shall I wander?
Upstairs and downstairs,
And in my lady's chamber.

DICKORY, DICKORY, DARE

Dickory, dickory, dare,
The pig flew up in the air;
The man in brown soon brought him down,
Dickory, dickory, dare.

HOT-CROSS BUNS!

Hot-cross buns! Hot-cross buns!
One a penny, two a penny, hot-cross buns.
If you have no daughters, give them to your sons.
One a penny, two a penny, hot-cross buns.

SEE-SAW, MARGERY DAW

See-saw, Margery Daw,
Jenny shall have a new master;
She shall have but a penny a day,
Because she can't work any faster.

LUCY LOCKET

Lucy Locket lost her pocket,
Kitty Fisher found it;
There was not a penny in it,
But a ribbon round it.

MY MAID MARY

My maid Mary, she minds the dairy,
    While I go hoeing and mowing each morn;
Gaily run the reel and the little spinning wheel,
    While I am singing and mowing my corn.

SING A SONG OF SIXPENCE

Sing a song of sixpence,
   A pocket full of rye;
Four-and-twenty blackbirds
   Baked in a pie.
When the pie was opened
   The birds began to sing;
Wasn't that a dainty dish
   To set before the King?

The King was in the countinghouse,
   Counting out his money;
The Queen was in the parlor,
   Eating bread and honey
The maid was in the garden,
   Hanging out the clothes;
When down came a blackbird
   And snipped off her nose.

TWO GRAY KITS

Two gray kits and the gray kits' mother
All went over the bridge together.
The bridge broke down, they all fell in;
"May the rats go with you," says Tom Bolin.

AS I WAS GOING TO ST. IVES

As I was going to St. Ives,
    I met a man with seven wives.

Every wife had seven sacks,
    Every sack had seven cats,

        Every cat had seven kits.
          Kits, cats, sacks and wives,

How many were going to St. Ives?

PUSSY CAT, PUSSY CAT

"Pussy Cat, Pussy Cat,
Where have you been?"
"I've been to London
To look at the Queen."

"Pussy Cat, Pussy Cat,
What did you there?"
"I frightened a little mouse
Under the chair."

PUSSY CAT SITS BY THE FIRE

Pussy Cat sits by the fire;
How did she come there?
In walks little doggy,
Says, "Pussy, are you there?
How do you do, Mistress Pussy?
Mistress Pussy, how d'ye do?"
"I thank you kindly, little dog,
I fare as well as you!"

PUSSY CAT ATE THE DUMPLINGS

Pussy Cat ate the dumplings, the dumplings,
Pussy Cat ate the dumplings.
Mama stood by, and cried, "Oh, fie!
Why did you eat the dumpling?"

DING, DONG, BELL!

Ding, dong, bell!
Pussy's in the well!
Who put her in?
Little Johnny Green
Who pulled her out?
Little Johnny Stout.

What a naughty boy was that
To try to drown poor pussy cat
Which never did him any harm,
But killed the mice in his father's barn!

A CAT CAME FIDDLING

A cat came fiddling out of a barn,
With a pair of bagpipes under her arm;
She could sing nothing but fiddle-de-dee,
The mouse has married the bumblebee;
Pipe, cat; dance, mouse--
We'll have a wedding at our good house.

THE CATS OF KILKENNY

There were once two cats of Kilkenny,
Each thought there was one cat too many;
So they fought and they fit,
And they scratched and they bit,
Till, excepting their nails
And the tips of their tails,
Instead of two cats, there weren't any.

THE CATS' SERENADE

The cats went out to serenade,
And on a banjo sweetly played;
And summer nights they climbed a tree,
And sang, "My love, oh, come to me!"

21

THE DEATH OF COCK ROBIN

Who killed Cock Robin?
"I," said the sparrow,
"With my bow and arrow,
I killed Cock Robin."

Who saw him die?
"I," said the fly,
"With my little eye,
I saw him die."

Who caught his blood?
"I," said the fish,
"With my little dish,
I caught his blood."

Who made his shroud?
"I," said the beetle,
"With my thread and needle,
I made his shroud."

Who'll be the clerk?
"I," said the lark,
"If it's not in the dark,
I'll be the clerk."

Who'll dig his grave?
"I," said the owl,
"With my spade and trowel,
I'll dig his grave."

Who'll be the parson?
"I," said the rook,
"With my little book,
I'll be the parson."

Who'll sing a psalm?
"I," said the thrush,
"As I sit in a bush,
I'll sing a psalm."

Who'll be chief mourner?
"I," said the dove,
"I mourn for my love,
I'll be chief mourner."

Who'll toll the bell?
"I," said the bull,
"Because I can pull,
I'll toll the bell."

All the birds of the air
Fell sighing and sobbing,
When they heard the bell toll
For poor Cock Robin.

Where, O Where

Where, O where, has my little dog gone?
O where, O where, can he be?

With his tail cut short, and his ears cut long--
O where, O where, has he gone?

SING SONG! MERRY GO ROUND

Sing song! merry go round,
Here we go up to the moon, O!
Little Johnny a penny has found,
And so we'll sing a tune, O!

"What shall I buy?"
Johnny did cry,
"With the penny I've found
So bright and round?"

What shall you buy?
A kite that will fly
Up to the moon,
All through the sky!

But if when it gets there,
It should stay in the air
Or the man in the moon
Should open the door,
And take it in with his long, long paw,
We should sing to another tune, O!

ONE, TWO,
BUCKLE MY SHOE

One, two, buckle my shoe;

Three, four, shut the door;

Five, six, pick up sticks;

Seven, eight, lay them straight;

Nine, ten, a good fat hen;

Eleven, twelve, dig and delve;

Thirteen, fourteen, maids are courting;

Fifteen, sixteen, maids in the kitchen;

Seventeen, eighteen, maids are waiting;

Nineteen, twenty, my platter's empty.

23

Father, May I Go to War?

Father, may I go to war?
Yes, you may, my son;
Wear your woolen comforter,
But don't fire off your gun.

I Won't Be My Father's Jack

I won't be my father's Jack,
I won't be my mother's Jill,
I will be the fiddler's wife,
And have music when I will.

The Cock Doth Crow

The cock doth crow
To let you know
If you be wise,
'Tis time to rise.

Little Sally Waters

Little Sally Waters, sitting in the sun,
Crying and weeping for a young man.
Rise, Sally, rise, wipe off your eyes;
Fly to the east, fly to the west,
Fly to the one that you love best.

The Greedy Man

The greedy man is he who sits
And bites bits out of plates
Or else takes up an almanac
And gobbles all the dates.

Burnie Bee

Burnie bee, burnie bee,
Tell me when your wedding be?
If it be tomorrow day,
Take your wings and fly away.

John Fought for His Beloved Land

John fought for his beloved land,
And when the war was over,
He kept a little cooky stand
And lived and died in clover.

Gray Goose and Gray Gander

Gray goose and gray gander,
Waft your wings together
And carry the good king's daughter
Over the one stand river.

Friday Night's Dream

Friday night's dream
On Saturday told
Is sure to come true,
Be it never so old.

Little Maiden

Little Maiden, better tarry;
Time enough next year to marry.
Hearts may change,
And so may fancy;
Wait a little longer, Nancy.

JACK and JILL

Jack and Jill went up the hill
To fetch a pail of water;
Jack fell down and broke his crown,
And Jill came tumbling after

Then up Jack got, and home did trot,
As fast as he could caper.
They put him to bed and plastered his head
With vinegar and brown paper.

THREE JOVIAL HUNTSMEN

There were three jovial huntsmen,
As I have heard them say,
And they would go a-hunting
Upon St. David's Day.

All day they hunted,
And nothing could they find,
But a ship a-sailing,
A-sailing with the wind.

One said it was a ship,
The other he said, Nay;
The third said it was a house,
With the chimney blown away

And all the night they hunted,
And nothing could they find
But the moon a-gliding,
A-gliding with the wind.

One said it was the moon,
The other he said, Nay;
The third said it was a cheese,
And half o't cut away.

And all the day they hunted,
And nothing did they find
But a hedgehog in a bramble-bush,
And that they left behind.

The first said it was a hedgehog,
The second he said, Nay;
The third said it was a pin cushion,
And the pins stuck in wrong way.

And all the night they hunted,
And nothing could they find
But a hare in a turnip-field,
And that they left behind.

The first said it was a hare,
The second he said, Nay;
The third said it was a calf,
And the cow had run away.

And all the day they hunted,
And nothing could they find
But an owl in a holly-tree,
And that they left behind.

One said it was an owl,
The second he said, Nay;
The third said 'twas an old man,
And his beard was growing gray.

I Have a Little Sister
(A Riddle)

I have a little sister, they call her peep, peep,
She wades the waters deep, deep, deep:
She climbs the mountains high, high, high;
Poor little creature, she has but one eye.
(A star.)

Old Mother Twitchett
(A Riddle)

Old Mother Twitchett had but one eye
And a long tail which she let fly;
And every time she went through a gap,
A bit of her tail she left in a trap.
(A needle.)

FOUR AND TWENTY
TAILORS

Four and twenty tailors went to kill a snail,
The best man among them durst not touch her tail;
She put out her horns like a little Kyloe cow—
Run, tailors, run, or she'll kill you all e'en now.

THERE WAS A JOLLY MILLER

There was a jolly miller
Lived on the river Dee;
He worked and sang from morn till night,
No lark so blithe as he.

And this the burden of his song
Forever used to be--
"I care for nobody-- no! not I,
Since nobody cares for me."

YET DIDN'T YOU SEE

Yet didn't you see, yet didn't you see,
What naughty tricks they put upon me?
They broke my pitcher,
And spilt my water,
And buffed my mother,
And chid my daughter,
And kissed my sister instead of me.

GILLY SILLY JARTER

Gilly Silly Jarter,
Who has lost a garter,
In a shower of rain;
The miller found it,
The miller ground it,
And the miller gave it to Silly again.

THE LITTLE MICE

This little mousie peeped within;
This little mousie walked right in!
This little mousie came to play;
This little mousie ran away!
This little mousie cried, "Dear me!
Dinner is done and it's time for tea!"

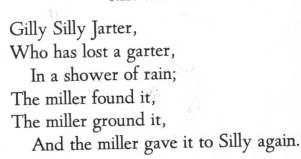

THE HUNTER OF REIGATE

A man went a-hunting at Reigate,
And wished to leap over a high gate.
Says the owner, "Go round,
With your gun and your hound,
For you never shall jump over my gate."

AS I WAS GOING ALONG

As I was going along, long, long,
A-singing a comical song, song, song,
The lane that I went was long, long, long,
And the song that I sung was a long, long song,
And so I went singing along.

THE MUFFIN MAN

O do you know the muffin man,
The muffin man, the muffin man,
O do you know the muffin man,
That lives in Drury Lane ?

O yes, I know the muffin man,
The muffin man, the muffin man,
O yes, I know the muffin man,
That lives in Drury Lane.

TO MARKET, TO MARKET

To market, to market to buy a fat pig,
    Home again, home again, jiggety-jig;

To market, to market to buy a fat hog,
    Home again, home again, jiggety-jog.

To market, to market to buy a plum bun,
    Home again, home again, market is done.

OLD TOBY SIZER

Old Toby Sizer is such a miser,
No cloak he'll buy to keep him dry, sir.
He'll not permit his neighbor, Randal,
To light his pipe by his short candle,
For fear, he says, he might convey
A little bit of light away.

WILLY, WILLY WILKIN

Willy, Willy Wilkin
Kissed the maids a-milking,
    Fa, la, la!
And with his merry daffing
He set them all a-laughing,
    Ha, ha, ha!

JOSHUA LANE

"I know I have lost my train,"
Said a man named Joshua Lane;
"But I'll run on the rails
With my coattails for sails
And maybe I'll catch it again."

PITTY PATTY POLT

Pitty Patty Polt,
Shoe the wild colt;
Here a nail,
And there a nail,
Pitty Patty Polt.

DOODLE DOODLE DOO

Doodle doodle doo,
The Princess lost her shoe:
Her Highness hopped--
The fiddler stopped,
Not knowing what to do.

THE CAT AND THE FIDDLE

Hey, diddle, diddle!
   The cat and the fiddle,
The cow jumped over the moon;
   The little dog laughed to see such sport,
And the dish ran away with the spoon.

A LITTLE PIG

A little pig found a fifty-dollar note
And purchased a hat and a very fine coat,
   With trousers and stockings and shoes,
Cravat, and shirt-collar, and gold-headed cane;
Then proud as could be, did he march up the lane,
   Says he, "I shall hear all the news."

LITTLE QUEEN PIPPIN

Little Queen Pippin once built a hotel,
How long and how high, I'm sure I can't tell;
The walls were of sugar, as white as the snow,
And jujube windows were placed in a row;
The columns were candy, and all very tall,
And a roof of choice cakes was spread over all.

I SAW AN OLD MAN

I saw an old man put shells in his pocket,
And up to the sky he went like a rocket;
But what he did there I could not but wonder,
As while I yet looked I thought I heard thunder.

"Old fellow, old fellow, old fellow," cried I,
"Oh whither, oh whither, oh whither so high?"
"The moon is green cheese, which I go to bring.
One half is for you, the rest for the king!"

RIDE A COCK-HORSE

Ride a cock-horse to Banbury Cross,
    To see an old lady upon a white horse;
Rings on her fingers and bells on her toes,
    She shall have music wherever she goes.

Ride a cock-horse to Banbury Cross,
    To see what Tommy can buy.
A penny white loaf, a penny white cake,
    And a two-penny apple pie!

HICKLE THEM, PICKLE THEM

Hickle them, pickle them,
Catch them and tickle them;
I'll teach the villains to eat my fine pears!
Gobble them, hobble them,
Snatch them and bobble them,
Till all of them fancy they have fallen downstairs.

TWEEDLE-DUM AND

Tweedle-dum and Tweedle-dee
Resolved to have a battle,
For Tweedle-dum said Tweedle-dee
Had spoiled his nice new rattle.

Just then flew by a monstrous crow,
As big as a tar-barrel,
Which frightened both the heroes so,
They quite forgot their quarrel.

OVER THE WATER

Over the water and over the sea,
And over the water to Charley.
I'll have none of your nasty beef,
Nor I'll have none of your barley;
But I'll have some of your very best flour
To make a white cake for my Charley.

TWEEDLE-DEE

31

The schoolroom clock

There's a neat little clock--
In the schoolroom it stands--
And it points to the time
With its two little hands.

And may we, like the clock,
Keep a face clean and bright,
With hands ever ready
To do what is right.

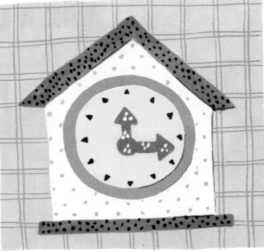

Dame Trot

Dame Trot and her cat
Led a peaceful life,
When they were not troubled
With other folks' strife.

When Dame had her dinner,
Pussy would wait,
And was sure to receive
A nice piece from her plate.

Ride away, ride

Ride away, ride away,
Johnny shall ride,
And he shall have Pussy Cat
Tied to one side;
And he shall have little dog
Tied to the other,
And Johnny shall ride
To see his grandmother.

Whistle, daughter, whistle

Whistle, daughter, whistle;
Whistle, daughter, dear.
I cannot whistle, mammy,
I cannot whistle clear.

Whistle, daughter, whistle,
Whistle for a pound.
I cannot whistle, mammy,
I cannot make a sound.

Twinkle, twinkle, little star

Twinkle, twinkle, little star,
How I wonder what you are!
Up above the world so high,
Like a diamond in the sky.

When the blazing sun is gone,
When he nothing shines upon,
Then you show your little light
Twinkle, twinkle, all the night.

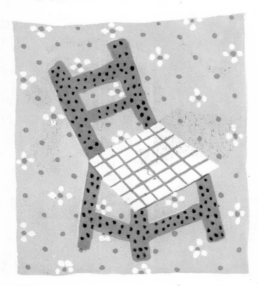

Old chairs to mend

If I'd as much money as I could spend,
I never would cry old chairs to mend;
Old chairs to mend, old chairs to mend;
I never would cry old chairs to mend.

If I'd as much money as I could tell,
I never would cry old clothes to sell;
Old clothes to sell, old clothes to sell;
I never would cry old clothes to sell.

Matthew, Mark, Luke and John

Matthew, Mark, Luke, and John,
Bless the bed that I lie on!
All four corners round about,
When I get in, when I get out.

Four corners to my bed,
Four angels round my head;
One to watch and one to pray,
And two to bear my soul away.

A family drive

Old Bob, young Bob,
Little Bob and big,
Molly Bob and Polly Bob,
And Polly Bobby's pig,
All went for a drive one day
And, strange as it may seem,
They drove six miles and back again
And never hurt the team.

Poor old Robinson Crusoe!

Poor old Robinson Crusoe!
Poor old Robinson Crusoe!
   They made him a coat
   Of an old nanny goat.
I wonder why they should do so!
   With a ring-a-ting-tang,
   And a ring-a-tang-ting,
Poor old Robinson Crusoe!

Dance to your daddie

Dance to your daddie,
My bonnie laddie;
Dance to your daddie,
My bonnie lamb;
You shall have a fishy,
On a little dishy;
You shall have a fishy,
When the boat comes home.

Mary had a pretty bird

Mary had a pretty bird,
   Feathers bright and yellow,
Slender legs—upon my word,
   He was a pretty fellow.

The sweetest notes he always sang,
   Which much delighted Mary;
And near the cage she'd ever sit,
   To hear her own canary.

The north wind

The north wind doth blow,
And we shall have snow,
And what will the robin do then,
   Poor thing?

He'll sit in the barn
And keep himself warm,
And hide his head under his wing,
   Poor thing!

33

TAFFY WAS A WELSHMAN

Taffy was a Welshman, Taffy was a thief;
Taffy came to my house and stole a piece of beef.

I went to Taffy's house, Taffy was not home;
Taffy came to my house and stole a marrow bone.

I went to Taffy's house, Taffy was not in;
Taffy came to my house and stole a silver pin.

I went to Taffy's house, Taffy was in bed;
I took up the marrow bone and beat him on the head.

A B C TUMBLE-DOWN D

A, B, C, tumble-down D,
The cat's in the cupboard and can't see me.

FEARS AND TEARS

Tommy's tears and Mary's fears
Will make them old before their years.

DOCTOR FOSTER

Doctor Foster went to Glo'ster
  In a shower of rain;
He stepped in a puddle, up to his middle,
And never went there again.

THIS LITTLE MAN

This little man lived all alone,
  And he was a man of sorrow;
For, if the weather was fair today,
  He was sure it would rain tomorrow.

THE OLD WOMAN

There was an old woman
  Lived under a hill;
And if she's not gone,
  She lives there still.

DEEDLE, DEEDLE, DUMPLING

Deedle, deedle, dumpling, my son John,
He went to bed with his stockings on;
One shoe off, and one shoe on;
Deedle, deedle, dumpling, my son John.

CATCH HIM, CROW!

Catch him, crow! carry him, kite!
Take him away till the apples are ripe;
When they are ripe and ready to fall,
Home comes Johnny, apples and all.

BELL-HORSES

Bell-horses, Bell-horses,
What time of day?
One o'clock, two o'clock,
Off and away!

BLOW, WIND, BLOW!

Blow, wind, blow! and go, mill, go!
That the miller may grind his corn;
That the baker may take it,
And into rolls make it,
And send us some hot in the morn.

THE HOUSE
That Jack Built

This is the house
that Jack built.

This is the malt
That lay in the house
that Jack built.

This is the rat
That ate the malt
That lay in the house
that Jack built.

This is the cat
That killed the rat
That ate the malt
That lay in the house
that Jack built.

This is the dog
That worried the cat
That killed the rat
That ate the malt
That lay in the house
that Jack built.

This is the maiden
all forlorn,
That milked the cow
with the crumpled horn,
That tossed the dog
That worried the cat
That killed the rat
That ate the malt
That lay in the house
that Jack built.

This is the cow
with the crumpled horn,
That tossed the dog
That worried the cat
That killed the rat
That ate the malt
That lay in the house
that Jack built.

This is the man
    all tattered and torn,
That kissed the maiden
    all forlorn,
That milked the cow
    with the crumpled horn,
That tossed the dog
That worried the cat
That killed the rat
That ate the malt
That lay in the house
    that Jack built.

This is the priest
    all shaven and shorn,
That married the man
    all tattered and torn,
That kissed the maiden
    all forlorn,
That milked the cow
    with the crumpled horn,
That tossed the dog
That worried the cat
That killed the rat
That ate the malt
That lay in the house
    that Jack built.

This is the cock
    that crowed in the morn,
That waked the priest
    all shaven and shorn,
That married the man
    all tattered and torn,
That kissed the maiden
    all forlorn,
That milked the cow
    with the crumpled horn,
That tossed the dog
That worried the cat
That killed the rat
That ate the malt
That lay in the house
    that Jack built.

This is the farmer
    sowing the corn,
That kept the cock
    that crowed in the morn,
That waked the priest
    all shaven and shorn,
That married the man
    all tattered and torn,
That kissed the maiden
    all forlorn,
That milked the cow
    with the crumpled horn,
That tossed the dog
That worried the cat
That killed the rat
That ate the malt
That lay in the house
    that Jack built.

37

3 Wise Men of Gotham

Three wise men of Gotham
Went to sea in a bowl;
If the bowl had been stronger,
My story would have been longer.

King Boggen's Hall

King Boggen, he built a fine new hall:
Pastry and piecrust, that was the wall;
The windows were made of black pudding and white,
Slated with pancakes,--you ne'er saw the like.

Upstairs, Downstairs

Upstairs, downstairs, upon my lady's window,
There I saw a cup of sack and a race of ginger,
Apples at the fire and nuts to crack,
A little boy in the cream-pot up to his neck.

Little Betty Winckle

Little Betty Winckle, she had a little pig.
It was a little pig, not very big;
When he was alive, he lived in clover,
But now he is dead, and that's all over.

Johnny Winckle, he sat down and cried.
Betty Winckle, she lay down and died.
So there was an end of one, two and three:
Johnny Winckle, he--
Betty Winckle, she--
and Piggie Wiggie.

38

The Little Man with a Gun

There was a little man, and he had a little gun,
And his bullets were made of lead, lead, lead;
He went to the brook, and saw a little duck,
And shot it through the head, head, head.

He carried it home to his old wife Joan,
And bade her a fire to make, make, make;
To roast the little duck, while he went to the brook,
To shoot and kill the drake, drake, drake.

The little drake was swimming, with his little curly tail,
And the little man made it his mark, mark, mark;
He let off his gun, but he fired too soon,
And away flew the drake with a quack, quack, quack.

WHEN I WAS A BACHELOR

When I was a bachelor I lived by myself,
And all the bread and cheese I got I laid upon the shelf.
The rats and the mice, they made such a strife,
I had to go to London to buy me a wife.

The streets were so wide and the lanes were so narrow,
I had to bring my wife home in a wheelbarrow.
The wheelbarrow broke, and my wife had a fall;
Down came wheelbarrow, little wife and all.

JOHN COOK'S LITTLE GRAY MARE

John Cook, he had a little gray mare;
 Hee, haw, hum.
Her legs were long and her back was bare,
 Hee, haw, hum.

John Cook was riding up Shooter's Bank,
 Hee, haw, hum.
The mare she began to kick and to prank,
 Hee, haw, hum.

John Cook was riding up Shooter's Hill,
 Hee, haw, hum.
His mare fell down and made her will,
 Hee, haw, hum.

The bridle and saddle were laid on the shelf,
 Hee, haw, hum.
If you want any more, you may sing it yourself,
 Hee, haw, hum.

39

HUSH-A-BYE, BABY

Hush-a-bye, baby,
Daddy is near;
Mamma is a lady,
And that's very clear.

ELSIE MARLEY

Elsie Marley is grown so fine
She won't get up to feed the swine,
But lies in bed till eight or nine,
And surely she does take her time.

A JOLLY FAT MILLER

A jolly fat miller is Poopleton Bun,
With elephant legs that weigh half a ton,
And a face that is round and red as the sun.

LITTLE JUMPING JOAN

Here am I, little jumping Joan;
When nobody's with me,
I'm always alone.

PLAY DAYS

How many days has my baby to play?
Saturday, Sunday, Monday,
Tuesday, Wednesday, Thursday, Friday,
Saturday, Sunday, Monday.

RING A RING O' ROSES

Ring a ring o' roses,
    A pocket full of posies.
Tisha! Tisha!
    We all fall down.

HIGH, DIDDLE DOUBT

High, diddle doubt, my candle's out!
My little maid is not at home;
Saddle my hog and bridle my dog,
And fetch my little maid home.

HUSH-A-BYE

Hush-a-bye, baby, lie still with thy daddy;
Thy mammy has gone to the mill
To get some wheat to make some meat,
So pray, my dear baby lie still.

IF WISHES WERE HORSES

If wishes were horses,
Beggars would ride;
If turnips were watches,
I'd wear one by my side.

HINKS MINX!

Hinks minx! the old witch winks,
The fat begins to fry;
There's nobody home but jumping Joan,
Father, Mother and I.

LONDON BRIDGE

London Bridge is falling down,
  Falling down, falling down.
London Bridge is falling down,
  My fair lady.

Build it up with iron bars,
  Iron bars, iron bars,
Build it up with iron bars,
  My fair lady.

Iron bars will bend and break,
  Bend and break, bend and break,
Iron bars will bend and break,
  My fair lady.

Build it up with needles and pins, etc.

Pins and needles rust and bend, etc.

Build it up with penny loaves, etc.

Penny loaves will tumble down, etc.

Build it up with gold and silver, etc.

Gold and silver I've not got, etc.

Here's a prisoner I have got, etc.

What's the prisoner done to you, etc.

Stole my watch and broke my crown, etc.

What'll you take to set him free, etc.

One hundred pounds will set him free, etc.

One hundred pounds we have not got, etc.

Then off to prison you must go, etc.

YOU RIDE BEHIND

You ride behind and I'll ride before,
And trot, trot away to Baltimore.
You shall take bread and I will take honey,
And both of us carry a purse full of money.

Lavender Blue

Lavender's blue, dilly, dilly, lavender's green;
When I am king, dilly, dilly, you shall be queen.
Call up your men, dilly, dilly, set them to work,
Some to the plow, dilly, dilly, some to the cart;
Some to make hay, dilly, dilly, some to cut corn,
While you and I, dilly, dilly, keep ourselves warm.

I HAD A LITTLE NUT TREE

I had a little nut tree; nothing would it bear
But a silver nutmeg and a golden pear.
The King of Spain's daughter came to visit me,
And all was because of my little nut tree.
I skipped over water, I danced over sea,
And all the birds in the air couldn't catch me.

42

Handy Spandy

Handy Spandy, Jack-a-dandy,
Loves plum cake and sugar candy.
He bought some at the grocer's shop
And out he came, hop, hop, hop!

A dillar, a dollar

A dillar, a dollar,
   A ten-o'clock scholar,
What makes you come so soon?
   You used to come at ten o'clock,
And now you come at noon.

I had a little moppet

I had a little moppet,
I put it in my pocket,
And fed it with corn and hay.
There came a proud beggar,
And swore he would have her,
And stole little moppet away.

Intery, mintery, cuttery, corn

Intery, mintery, cuttery, corn,
Apple seed and apple thorn;
Wire, brier, limber-lock,
Five geese in a flock;
Sit and sing by a spring,
O-U-T and in again.

How many miles to Babylon?

How many miles to Babylon?
   Threescore miles and ten.
Can I get there by candlelight?
   Yes, and back again.
If your heels are nimble and light,
You may get there by candlelight.

ROBIN HOOD

Robin Hood, Robin Hood,
  Is in the mickle wood!
Little John, Little John,
  He to the town is gone.

Robin Hood, Robin Hood,
  Is telling his beads,
All in the greenwood,
  Among the green weeds.

Little John, Little John,
  If he comes no more,
Robin Hood, Robin Hood,
  He will fret full sore!

I HAD A LITTLE PONY

I had a little pony,
    His name was Dapple-Gray;
I lent him to a lady
    To ride a mile away.

She whipped him, she slashed him,
    She rode him through the mire;
I would not lend my pony now
    For all the lady's hire.

I HAD A LITTLE CASTLE

I had a little castle upon the sea sand,
One half was water, the other was land;
I opened my little castle door, and guess what I found;
I found a fair lady with a cup in her hand.
The cup was golden, filled with wine;
Drink, fair lady, and thou shalt be mine!

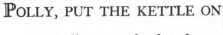

POLLY, PUT THE KETTLE ON

Polly, put the kettle on,
Polly, put the kettle on,
Polly, put the kettle on,
We'll all have tea.

Sukey, take it off again,
Sukey, take it off again,
Sukey, take it off again,
They've all gone away.

THREE BLIND MICE

Three blind mice!   Three blind mice!
See how they run!   See how they run!
They all ran after the farmer's wife;
She cut off their tails with a carving knife.
Did you ever see such a sight in your life
As three blind mice?

A Farmer Went Trotting

A farmer went trotting upon his gray mare,
    Bumpety, bumpety, bump!
With his daughter behind him so rosy and fair,
    Lumpety, lumpety, lump!

A raven cried croak! and they all tumbled down,
    Bumpety, bumpety, bump!
The mare broke her knees and the farmer his crown,
    Lumpety, lumpety, lump!

The mischievous raven flew laughing away.
    Bumpety, bumpety, bump!
And vowed he would serve them the same the next day,
    Lumpety, lumpety, lump!

THREE LITTLE KITTENS

Three little kittens, they lost their mittens, and they began to cry,
　　"Oh, mother dear, we sadly fear
　　Our mittens we have lost!"

"What! lost your mittens, you naughty kittens!
　　Then you shall have no pie."
　　"Meow, meow, meow!"

The three little kittens found their mittens, and they began to cry,
　　"Oh! mother dear, see here, see here,
　　Our mittens we have found."

"What! found your mittens, you good little kittens,
　　Then you shall have some pie."
　　"Purr, purr, purr."

The three little kittens put on their mittens and soon ate up the pie.
　　"Oh! mother dear, we greatly fear
　　Our mittens we have soiled."

"What! soiled your mittens, you naughty kittens!"
　　Then they began to sigh,
　　"Meow, meow, meow!"

The three little kittens washed their mittens, and hung them up to
　　dry.
　　"Oh! mother dear, look here, look here,
　　Our mittens we have washed."

"What! washed your mittens, you darling kittens!
　　But I smell a rat close by!
　　Hush! hush! hush!"

January brings the snow,
Makes our feet and fingers glow.

February brings the rain,
Thaws the frozen lake again.

March brings breezes loud and shrill,
Stirs the dancing daffodil.

April brings the primrose sweet,
Scatters daisies at our feet.

May brings flocks of pretty lambs.
Skipping by their fleecy dams.

June brings tulips, lilies, roses,
Fills the children's hands with posies.

It's Raining

It's raining, it's pouring,
The old man is snoring.

The First of May

The fair maid who, the first of May
Goes to the fields at break of day,
And washes in dew from the hawthorn tree,
Will ever after handsome be.

March Winds

March winds and April showers
Bring forth May flowers.

Summer Breeze

Summer breeze, so softly blowing,
In my garden pinks are growing;
If you go and send the showers,
You may come and smell my flowers.

I've Got a Rocket

I've got a rocket in my pocket,
I cannot stop to play;
Away she goes, I've burnt my toes,
It's Independence Day!

Mother Goose

Hot July brings cooling showers,
Apricots and gillyflowers.

August brings the sheaves of corn,
Then the harvest home is borne.

Warm September brings the fruit,
Sportsmen then begin to shoot.

Fresh October brings the pheasant,
Then to gather nuts is pleasant.

Dull November brings the blast,
Then the leaves are whirling fast.

Chill December brings the sleet,
Blazing fire and Christmas treat.

Harvest Home
Harvest home, harvest home,
Ne'er a load's been overthrown.

Thirty Days Hath September

Thirty days hath September,
April, June and November;
All the rest have thirty-one,
February has twenty-eight alone,
Except in Leap Year.   That's the time
When February's days are twenty-nine.

Rain, Rain, Go Away
Rain, rain, go away,
Come again another day;
Little Tommy wants to play.

The North Winds Blow
Cold and raw the north winds blow,
Bleak in the mornings early;
All the hills are covered with snow,
And winter's now come fairly.

Christmas Is Coming
Christmas is coming, the geese are getting fat;
Please to put a penny in the old man's hat;
If you haven't got a penny, a ha'penny will do.
If you haven't got a ha'penny, God bless you.

A Duck and a Drake

A duck and a drake,
And a halfpenny cake,
With a penny to pay the old baker.

A hop and a scotch
In another notch,
Slitherum, slatherum, take her.

I'll Sing You a Song

I'll sing you a song--
Though not very long,
Yet I think it as pretty as any;
Put your hand in your purse,
You'll never be worse,
And give the poor singer a penny.

Tommy Tonsey

Tommy Tonsey's come from France,
Where he learned the latest dance;
He has brought a scarlet dog,
And now the town is all agog.

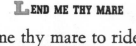

Little Miss Muffet

Little Miss Muffet
She sat on a tuffet,
Eating of curds and whey;
There came a great spider,
Who sat down beside her,
And frightened Miss Muffet away.

Doctor Fell

I do not like thee, Doctor Fell;
The reason why I cannot tell;
But this I know, and know full well,
I do not like thee, Doctor Fell!

Lend Me Thy Mare

'' Lend me thy mare to ride a mile?''
''She is lamed, leaping over a stile.''
''Alack! and I must keep the fair!
I'll give thee money for thy mare.''
''Oh, oh, say you so?
Money will make the mare to go!''

JACK SPRAT

Jack Sprat could eat no fat,
His wife could eat no lean,
And so between them both,
They licked the platter clean.
Jack Sprat, to live pretty,
Now bought him a pig;
It was not very little,
It was not very big.
It was not very lean,
It was not very fat.
"It will serve for a grunter,"
Said little Jack Sprat.

Jack Sprat bought a cow,
His Joan for to please;
For Joan she could make
Both butter and cheese,
Or pancakes or puddings
Without any fat;
A notable housewife
Was little Joan Sprat.

Now I have told you the story
Of little Jack Sprat,
And his little wife Joan,
And their cow and all that.
Now Jack has got rich,
And has plenty of pelf;
If you know any more,
You may tell it yourself.

Bobby Shaftoe has a Cow

Bobby Shaftoe has a cow,
Black and white about the mow;
Open the gates and let her through,
Bobby Shaftoe's own cow!
Bobby Shaftoe has a hen,
Cockle button, cockle ben,
She lays eggs for gentlemen,
But none for Bobby Shaftoe!

The Blacksmith

"Robert Barnes, my fellow fine,
Can you shoe this horse of mine?"
"Yes, good sir, that I can,
As well as any other man;
Here's a nail and there's a prod,
And now, good sir, your horse is shod."

Quite Well, Quite Hearty

A little girl quite well and hearty
Thought she'd like to give a party.
But as her friends were shy and wary,
Nobody came but her own canary.

Little Jack Horner

Little Jack Horner sat in the corner,
Eating a Christmas pie;
He put in his thumb, and he pulled out a plum,
And said, "What a good boy am I!"

Peter White

Peter White will never go right.
Do you know the reason why?
He follows his nose wherever he goes,
And that stands all awry.

John and Jane

As John and Jane walked through the lane,
One very pleasant Sunday,
Said John to Jane, "Unless it rain,
Tomorrow will be Monday."

Rock-a-Bye, Baby, on the Tree Top!

Rock-a-bye, baby, on the tree top!
When the wind blows the cradle will rock,
When the bough breaks the cradle will fall.
Down will come baby, bough, cradle and all.

One, he loves

One, he loves; two, he loves;
Three, he loves, they say.
Four, he loves with all his heart;
Five, he casts away.
Six, he loves; seven she loves;
Eight, they both love.
Nine, he comes; ten, he tarries;
Eleven, he courts; twelve, he marries.

Jerry Tigg's guinea pig

Whoop! little Jerry Tigg
Has got a guinea pig;
I wonder where he bought it!
And Jerry Tigg has taught it
To wear a purple wig,
And dance an Irish jig.

Give My Horse a Ton of Hay

Give my horse a ton of hay,
And put him in the stable;
And do your best the livelong day,
To make him comfortable.

Cushy cow

Cushy cow, bonny, let down thy milk,
And I will give thee a gown of silk;
A gown of silk and a silver tee,
If thou wilt let down thy milk to me.

Cobbler, Cobbler, Mend My Shoe

Cobbler, cobbler, mend my shoe;
Get it done by half past two.
Do it neat, and do it strong,
I will pay you when it's done.

Jenny Wren was wed

Jenny Wren last week was wed,
And built her nest in grandpa's shed;
Look in next week and you shall see
Two little eggs, and maybe three.

Molly, my sister, and I

Molly, my sister, and I fell out,
And what do you think it was all about?
She loved coffee and I loved tea,
And that was the reason we couldn't agree.

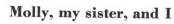

OLD MOTHER HUBBARD

Old Mother Hubbard
Went to the cupboard,
To get her poor dog a bone;
When she got there
The cupboard was bare,
And so the poor dog had none.

She went to the baker's
To buy him some bread,
But when she came back
The poor dog was dead.

She went to the joiner's
To buy him a coffin,
But when she came back
The poor dog was laughing.

She took a clean dish
To get him some tripe,
But when she came back
He was smoking his pipe.

She went to the hatter's
To buy him a hat,
But when she came back
He was feeding the cat.

She went to the barber's
To buy him a wig,
But when she came back
He was dancing a jig.

She went to the grocer's
To buy him some fruit,
But when she came back
He was playing the flute.

She went to the tailor's
To buy him a coat,
But when she came back
He was riding a goat.

She went to the cobbler's
To buy him some shoes,
But when she came back
He was reading the news.

She went to the sempstress
To buy him some linen,
But when she came back
The dog was spinning.

She went to the hosiers
To buy him some hose,
But when she came back
He was dressed in his clothes.

She went to the fishmonger's
To buy him some fish,
But when she came back
He was licking the dish.

The dame made a curtsey,
The dog made a bow;
The dame said, "Your servant;"
The dog said, "Bow-wow!"

THE QUEEN
OF HEARTS

The Queen of Hearts,
She made some tarts,
All on a summer's day.
The Knave of Hearts,
He stole the tarts,
And took them clean away.

The King of Hearts
Called for the tarts,
And beat the Knave full sore.
The Knave of Hearts
Brought back the tarts,
And vowed he'd steal no more.

HERE WE GO ROUND THE MULBERRY BUSH

Here we go round the mulberry bush,
  The mulberry bush, the mulberry bush,
Here we go round the mulberry bush,
  On a cold and frosty morning.

This is the way we wash our hands,
  Wash our hands, wash our hands,
This is the way we wash our hands,
  On a cold and frosty morning.

This is the way we wash our clothes,
  Wash our clothes, wash our clothes,
This is the way we wash our clothes,
  On a cold and frosty morning.

This is the way we go to school,
  Go to school, go to school,
This is the way we go to school,
  On a cold and frosty morning.

This is the way we come out of school,
  Come out of school, come out of school,
This is the way we come out of school,
  On a cold and frosty morning.

NIXIE DIXIE

Nixie, Dixie, hickory bow,
Thirteen Dutchmen in a row;
Two corporals hold a piece of twine,
To help the Dutchmen form a line.

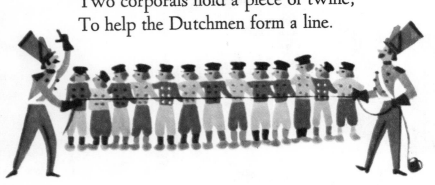

SNEEZING

If you sneeze on Monday, you sneeze for danger;
Sneeze on Tuesday, kiss a stranger;
Sneeze on Wednesday, sneeze for a letter;
Sneeze on Thursday, something better;
Sneeze on Friday, sneeze for sorrow;
Sneeze on Saturday, joy for tomorrow.

LITTLE BO-PEEP HAS LOST HER SHEEP

Little Bo-peep has lost her sheep,
And can't tell where to find them;
Leave them alone, and they'll come home,
And bring their tails behind them.

Little Bo-peep fell fast asleep,
And dreamt she heard them bleating;
But when she awoke, she found it a joke,
For they were still a-fleeting.

Then up she took her little crook,
Determined for to find them;
She found them indeed, but it made her heart bleed,
For they'd left their tails behind them.

It happened one day, as Bo-peep did stray
Over a meadow hard by,
That there she espied their tails, side by side,
All hung on a tree to dry.

She heaved a sigh, and gave by and by
Each careless sheep a banging;
And as for the rest, she thought it was best,
Just to leave the tails a-hanging.

BABY AND I

Baby and I
Were baked in a pie;
The gravy was wonderful hot:
We had nothing to pay
To the baker that day
And so we crept out of the pot.

SEE SAW, SACAR A DOWN

See saw, sacar a down,
Which is the way to Boston Town?
One foot up, the other foot down,
That is the way to Boston Town.

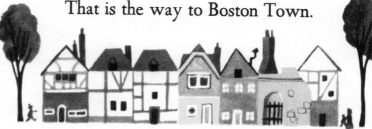

The Seasons

Spring is showery, flowery, bowery;
Summer: hoppy, croppy, poppy;
Autumn: wheezy, sneezy, freezy;
Winter: slippy, drippy, nippy.

Wash the Dishes

Wash the dishes, wipe the dishes,
Ring the bell for tea;
Three good wishes, three good kisses,
I will give to thee.

Miss Jane Had a Bag

Miss Jane had a bag, and a mouse was in it.
She opened the bag, he was out in a minute.
The cat saw him jump and run under the table,"
And the dog said, "Catch him, Puss, soon as you're able."

See, See!

See, see! What shall I see?
A horse's head where his tail should be.

Higher Than a House
(A Riddle)

Higher than a house, higher than a tree.
Oh! Whatever can that be?
(A star.)

Barber, Barber

Barber, barber, shave a pig.
How many hairs will make a wig?
Four and twenty; that's enough.
Give the barber a pinch of snuff.

Did You See My Wife?

Did you see my wife, did you see, did you see,
Did you see my wife, looking for me?
She wears a straw bonnet, with ribbons on it,
And dimity petticoats over her knee.

Around the Green Gravel

Around the green gravel the grass grows green,
And all the pretty maids are plain to be seen;
Wash them with milk, and clothe them in silk,
And write their names with a pen and ink.

Lovely Rainbow Hung So High

Lovely rainbow, hung so high,
Quite across the distant sky,
Please touch the ground close by my side,
And o'er your bridge I'll pony ride.

The Rose Is Red

The rose is red, the violet blue,
The gilly flower sweet—and so are you.
These are the words you bade me say
For a pair of new gloves on Easter day.

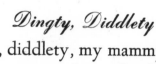

The Cock's on the Housetop

The cock's on the housetop blowing his horn;
The bull's in the barn a threshing of corn;
The maids in the meadows are making of hay;
The ducks in the river are swimming away.

The Man in the Moon

The Man in the Moon looked out of the moon,
And this is what he said,
" 'Tis time that, now I'm getting up,
All babies went to bed."

Dingty, Diddlety

Dingty, diddlety, my mammy's maid,
She stole oranges, I am afraid;
Some in her pocket, some in her sleeve,
She stole oranges, I do believe.

One, Two, Three, Four, Five

One, two, three, four, five,
Once I caught a fish alive.
Six, seven, eight, nine, ten,
I let it go again.
Why did you let it go?
Because it bit my finger so.
Which finger did it bite?
The little one upon the right.

When I Work in the House

When I work in the house I always say,
"How I'd like to toil out of doors all day!"
And when they send me to weed the flowers
The day seems made of a hundred hours!

Willy Boy

Willy Boy, Willy Boy, where are you going?
I will go with you, if that I may."
"I'm going to the meadow to see them a-mowing,
I'm going to help them make the hay."

Three Young Rats

Three young rats with black felt hats,
Three young ducks with new straw flats,
Three young dogs with curling tails,
Three young cats with demi-veils,
Went out to walk with two young pigs,
In satin vests and sorrel wigs;
But suddenly it chanced to rain,
And so they all went home again.

THE NEWS OF THE DAY

"What is the news of the day,
Good neighbor, I pray?"
"They say the balloon
Is gone up to the moon!"

TOMMY TROT

Tommy Trot, a man of law,
Sold his bed and lay on straw;
Sold the straw and slept on grass,
To buy his wife a looking-glass.

DAVY, DAVY, DUMPLING

Davy, Davy, Dumpling,
  Boil him in the pot;
Sugar him and butter him,
  And eat him while he's hot.

LITTLE TOMMY TITTLEMOUSE

Little Tommy Tittlemouse
Lived in a little house;
He caught fishes
In other men's ditches.

SEE A PIN

See a pin and pick it up,
All the day you'll have good luck.
See a pin and let it lay,
Bad luck you'll have all the day.

SMILING GIRLS, ROSY BOYS

Smiling girls, rosy boys,
Come and buy my little toys:
Monkeys made of gingerbread,
And sugar houses painted red.

THE FARMER IN THE DELL

The farmer in the dell,
The farmer in the dell,
Heigho! the derry oh,
The farmer in the dell.

The farmer takes a wife,
The farmer takes a wife,
Heigho! the derry oh,
The farmer takes a wife.

The wife takes the child,
The wife takes the child,
Heigho! the derry oh,
The wife takes the child.

The child takes the nurse, (etc.)

The nurse takes the dog, (etc.)

The dog takes the cat, (etc.)

The cat takes the rat, (etc.)

The rat takes the cheese, (etc.)

The cheese stands alone, (etc.)

Snail, Snail

Snail, snail, come out of your shell,
And show me what you have to sell;
And if your wares do please me well,
I'll take your shop, your dainty shell.

Pat-a-Cake

Pat-a-cake, pat-a-cake, baker's man!
Bake me a cake as fast as you can;
Roll it and pat it and mark it with "B,"
And put it in the oven for baby and me.

I SAW A SHIP A-SAILING

I saw a ship a-sailing,
A-sailing on the sea;
And, oh! it was all laden
With pretty things for thee!

There were comfits in the cabin,
And apples in the hold;
The sails were made of silk,
And the masts were made of gold.

The four-and-twenty sailors
That stood between the decks
Were four-and-twenty white mice
With chains about their necks.

The captain was a duck,
With a packet on his back;
And when the ship began to move,
The captain said, "Quack! quack!"

GIRLS AND BOYS, COME OUT TO PLAY

Girls and boys, come out to play,
The moon doth shine as bright as day;
Leave your supper and leave your sleep,
And come with your playfellows into the street.
Come with a whoop, come with a call,
Come with a good will or not at all.
Up the ladder and down the wall,
A halfpenny roll will serve us all.
You find milk, and I'll find flour,
And we'll have a pudding in half an hour.

THERE WAS AN OLD WOMAN

There was an old woman
    Tossed up in a basket,
Seventeen times as high as the moon;
    And where she was going,
I couldn't but ask it,
    For in her hand she carried a broom.

"Old woman, old woman, old woman," said I,
"O whither, O whither, O whither so high?"
"To sweep the cobwebs off the sky!
And I'll be with you by and by."

HARK! HARK!

Hark! Hark! The dogs do bark,
Beggars are coming to town;
Some in rags and some in tags,
And some in velvet gowns.

LITTLE POPPLE-DE-POLLY

Little Popple-de-Polly
Said, "See my new dolly!
    With her beautiful, pop-open eyes;
But I can't make her speak,
Though I've tried for a week;
    And whenever I hug her, she cries!"

HERE COMES A POOR WOMAN

Here comes a poor woman from baby-land,
With five small children on her hand;
One can brew, another can bake,
Another can make a pretty round cake.
One can sit in the garden and spin,
Another can make a fine bed for the king;
Pray, ma'am, will you take one in?

HUMPTY DUMPTY

Humpty Dumpty sat on a wall,
Humpty Dumpty had a great fall;

All the King's horses and all the King's men
Cannot put Humpty Dumpty together again.

61

Why may not I love Johnny

Johnny shall have a new bonnet,
And Johnny shall go to the fair,
And Johnny shall have a blue ribbon
To tie up his bonny brown hair.

And why may not I love Johnny?
And why may not Johnny love me?
And why may not I love Johnny
As well as another body?

And here's a leg for a stocking,
And here's a foot for a shoe,
And he has a kiss for his daddy,
And two for his mammy, I trow.

And why may not I love Johnny?
And why may not Johnny love me?
And why may not I love Johnny
As well as another body?

UP AT PICCADILLY, OH!

Up at Piccadilly, oh!
The coachman takes his stand,
And when he meets a pretty girl
He takes her by the hand;
Whip away forever, oh!
Drive away so clever, oh!
All the way to Bristol, oh!
He drives her four-in-hand.

WOULDN'T IT BE FUNNY?

Wouldn't it be funny--
    Wouldn't it now,--
If the dog said, "Moo-oo"
    And the cow said, "Bow-wow?"
If the cat sang and whistled,
    And the bird said, "Mia-ow?"
Wouldn't it be funny--
Wouldn't it now?

If all the seas

If all the seas were one sea,
What a great sea that would be!

If all the trees were one tree,
What a great tree that would be!

If all the axes were one axe,
What a great axe that would be!

were one sea

And if all the men were one man,
What a great man that would be!

And if the great man took the great axe
And cut down the great tree

And let it fall into the great sea,
What a splish splash that would be!

Billy, Billy, come and play

"Billy, Billy, come and play,
While the sun shines bright as day."

"Yes, my Polly, so I will,
For I love to please you still."

"Billy, Billy, have you seen
Sam and Betsy on the green?"

"Yes, my Polly, I saw them pass,
Skipping o'er the new-mown grass."

"Billy, Billy, come along,
And I will sing a pretty song."

"Oh, then, Polly, I'll make haste,
Not one moment will I waste,
But will come and hear you sing,
And my fiddle I will bring."

BOW-WOW, SAYS THE DOG

Bow-wow, says the dog;
Mew, mew, says the cat;
Grunt, grunt, goes the hog;
And squeak says the rat.
Tu-whu, says the owl;
Caw-caw, goes the crow;
Quack, quack, goes the duck;
And moo, says the cow.

A MILLION LITTLE DIAMONDS

A million little diamonds
   Twinkled on the trees;
And all the little maidens said,
   "A jewel, if you please!"
But while they held their hands outstretched,
   To catch the diamonds gay,
A million little sunbeams came,
   And stole them all away.

CRY, BABY, CRY

Cry, baby, cry,
Put your finger in your eye;
Then go and tell your mother it was not I.

JACK, BE NIMBLE

Jack, be nimble,
Jack, be quick,
Jack, jump over the candlestick.

THE SLIM LITTLE TINKER

The slim little tinker, Davy De Longs,
In body and legs is shaped like a tongs;
But birds stop their singing to hear
   his sweet songs.

LITTLE BLUE BEN

Little Blue Ben, that lives in the glen,
Keeps a blue cat and one blue hen,
Which laid of blue eggs a score and ten.
Where shall I find the little Blue Ben?

JOHNNY MORGAN

Little Johnny Morgan,
   Gentleman of Wales,
Came riding on a nanny goat,
   Selling of pigs' tails.

BABY, MY DOLLY

Baby, my dolly, oh, she never cries!
Lie still, my darling, and close little eyes!
Mother must go, dear, and look for the others--
All the dear sisters, and all the dear brothers.

AS I WAS GOING TO SELL MY EGGS

As I was going to sell my eggs,
I met a man with bandy legs,
Bandy legs and crooked toes,
I tripped up his heels, and he fell on his nose.

CURLY LOCKS! CURLY LOCKS!

Curly Locks! Curly Locks! wilt thou be mine?
Thou shalt not wash dishes, nor yet feed the swine;
But sit on a cushion, and sew a fine seam,
And feed upon strawberries, sugar and cream!

This is the way the ladies ride,
   Tri, tre, tri, tree, tri, tre, tri, tree!
This is the way the ladies ride,
   Tri, tre, tri, tree, tri, tre, tri, tree!

This is the way the gentlemen ride;
   Gallop-a-trot!   Gallop-a-trot!
This is the way the gentlemen ride;
   Gallop-a-trot!   Gallop-a-trot!

This is the way the farmers ride!
   Hobbledy-hoy, hobbledy-hoy!
This is the way the farmers ride!
   Hobbledy-hoy, hobbledy-hoy!

THIS IS THE WAY

THOMAS and ANNIS

Thomas and Annis met in the dark.
"Good morning," said Thomas.
"Good morning," said Annis.
And so they began to talk.
"I'll give you--" said Thomas;
"Give me!" said Annis,
"I prithee, love, tell me what?"
"Some nuts," said Thomas.
"Some nuts," said Annis,
"Nuts are good to crack."
"I love you," said Thomas.
"Love me!" said Annis,
"I prithee, Love, tell me where?"
"In my heart," said Thomas.
"In your heart!" said Annis,
"How come you to love me there?"
"I'll marry you," said Thomas.
"Marry me!" said Annis,
"I prithee, Love, tell me when."
"Next Sunday," said Thomas.
"Next Sunday!" said Annis,
"I wish next Sunday were come."

65

TEN LITTLE INJUNS

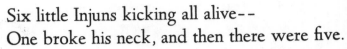

Ten little Injuns standing in a line--
One went home, and then there were nine.

Six little Injuns kicking all alive--
One broke his neck, and then there were five.

Five little Injuns on a cellar door--
One tumbled off, and then there were four.

Four little Injuns climbing up a tree--
One fell down, and then there were three.

Nine little Injuns swinging on a gate--
One tumbled off, and then there were eight.

Eight little Injuns never heard of heaven--
One kicked the bucket, and then there were seven.

Seven little Injuns cutting up tricks--
One went to bed, and then there were six.

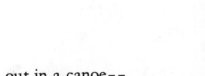

Three little Injuns out in a canoe--
One fell overboard, and then there were two.

Two little Injuns fooling with a gun--
One shot the other, and then there was one.

One little Injun living all alone--
He got married, and then there was none!

Mary had a little lamb,
Its fleece was white as snow,
And everywhere that Mary went
The lamb was sure to go.

It followed her to school one day,
Which was against the rule;
It made the children laugh and play
To see a lamb at school.

And so the teacher turned it out,
But still it lingered near,
And waited patiently about
Till Mary did appear.

And then it ran to her and laid
Its head upon her arm,
As if it said, "I'm not afraid --
You'll keep me from all harm."

"What makes the lamb love Mary so?"
The eager children cry.
"Why, Mary loves the lamb, you know,"
The teacher did reply.

LITTLE ROBIN REDBREAST

Little Robin Redbreast sat upon a rail;
Niddle-naddle went his head, wiggle-waggle went his tail.

Little Robin Redbreast sat upon a tree,
Up went Pussy Cat, and down went he.

Down came Pussy Cat, and away Robin ran;
Says little Robin Redbreast, "Catch me if you can."

Little Robin Redbreast jumped upon a wall;
Pussy Cat jumped after him, and almost got a fall.

Little Robin chirped and sang, and what did Pussy say?
Pussy Cat said, "Mew," and Robin jumped away.

CHRISTMAS GIFTS

A silver cup with a name upon it,
A china doll with muff and bonnet;
An old gray cat with pretty kittens;
A rabbit cape and scarlet mittens,
All these are on the Christmas tree
As gifts for baby and for me.

A Little Green Bird

A little green bird sat on a fence rail,
Chee-choo, chee-choo, chee!
Its song was the sweetest that ever I heard;
Chee-choo, chee-choo, chee!
I ran for some salt to put on its tail;
Chee-choo, chee-choo, chee!
But while I was gone, away flew the bird;
Chee-choo, chee-choo, chee!

There Was a Glossy Blackbird

There was a glossy blackbird once
   Lived in a cherry tree,
He chirped and sung from morn to night,
   No bird so blithe as he!

And this the burden of his song
   Forever used to be:
Good boys shall have cherries as soon as they're ripe,
   But naughty boys none from me.

There Was an Owl

There was an owl lived in an oak,
Wisky, wasky, weedle;
And every word he ever spoke
Was fiddle, faddle, feedle.

A gunner chanced to come this way,
Wisky, wasky, weedle;
Says he, "I'll shoot you, silly bird."
Fiddle, faddle, feedle.

Little Robin

Pit, pat, well-a-day!
Little Robin flew away;
Where can little Robin be?
Gone into the cherry tree.

Little Cock Robin

Little Cock Robin peeped out of his cabin
To see the cold weather come in.
Tit for tat, what matter for that?
He'll hide his head under his wing.

68

All of a Row

All of a row,
Bend the bow,
Shot at a pigeon
And killed a crow.

The Old Crow

There was an old crow
Sat upon a clod.
There's an end of my song.
That's very odd.

The Robins

A robin and a robin's son
Once went to town to buy a bun.
They couldn't decide on plum or plain,
And so they went back home again.

A Little Cock Sparrow

A little cock sparrow sat on a tree,
And he chirruped, he chirruped, so merry was he;
A naughty boy came with his wee bow and arrow,
Determined to shoot this little cock sparrow.

"This little cock sparrow shall make me a stew,
And his giblets shall make me a little pie, too."
"Oh, no," says the sparrow, "I won't make a stew."
So he flapped his wings and away he flew.

Two Wrens

Two wrens there were upon a tree:
Whistle and I'll come to thee;
Another came, and there were three:
Whistle and I'll come to thee;
Another came, and there were four.
You needn't whistle any more,
For, being frightened, off they flew,
And there are none to show to you.

What Shall I Do?

he dove says, "Coo, coo, what shall I do?
an scarce maintain two."
ooh! pooh!" says the wren, "I have got ten,
d I keep them all like gentlemen."

Simple Simon

Simple Simon met a pieman, going to the fair;
Says Simple Simon to the pieman, "Let me taste your ware."

Says the pieman to Simple Simon, "Show me first your penny."
Says Simple Simon to the pieman, "Indeed I have not any."

He went to catch a dickey bird, and thought he could not fail,
Because he'd got a little salt, to put upon his tail.

He went to take a bird's nest; 'twas built upon a bough;
A branch gave way and Simon fell into a dirty slough.

He went to shoot a wild duck, but the wild duck flew away;
Says Simon, "I can't hit him, because he will not stay."

He went for to eat honey, out of the mustard pot;
It bit his tongue until he cried; that was all the good he got.

Simple Simon went a-fishing for to catch a whale;
All the water he had got was in his mother's pail.

He went to ride a spotted cow, that had a little calf,
She threw him down upon the ground, which made the people
    laugh.

Simple Simon went to look if plums grew on a thistle;
He pricked his fingers very much, which made poor Simon
    whistle.

He went for water in a sieve, but soon it all ran through;
And now poor Simple Simon bids you all adieu.

GOOD KING ARTHUR

When good King Arthur ruled this land,
 He was a goodly king,
He bought three pecks of barley meal,
 To make a bag pudding..

A bag pudding the king did make,
 And stuffed it well with plums;
And in it put great lumps of fat,
 As big as my two thumbs.

The king and queen did eat thereof,
 And noblemen beside;
And what they could not eat that night,
 The queen next morning fried.

ONE MISTY, MOISTY MORNING

One misty, moisty morning,
  When cloudy was the weather,
I chanced to meet an old man
  Clothed all in leather;
He began to compliment,
  And I began to grin--
"How do you do?" and "How do you do?"
  And "How do you do?" again!

There Was an Old Woman as I've Heard Tell

There was an old woman, as I've heard tell,
She went to market, her eggs for to sell;
She went to market all on a market day,
And she fell asleep on the king's highway.

There came by a peddler whose name was Stout;
He cut her petticoats all round about;
He cut her petticoats up to the knees,
Which made the old woman to shiver and sneeze.

When this little woman first did wake,
She began to shiver and she began to shake;
She began to wonder and she began to cry,
"Oh! deary, deary, me, this is none of I!

"But if it be I, as I do hope it be,
I've a little dog at home, and he'll know me;
If it be I, he'll wag his little tail,
And if it be not I, he'll loudly bark and wail."

Home went the little woman all in the dark;
Up got the little dog, and he began to bark;
He began to bark, so she began to cry,
"Lack-a-mercy on me, this is none of I!"

NEEDLES AND PINS

Needles and pins, needles and pins,
When a man marries, his troubles begin.

JERRY HALL

Jerry Hall, he was so small,
A rat could eat him, hat and all.

MY FATHER HE DIED

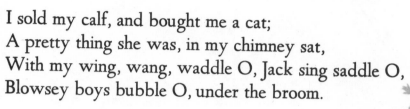

My father, he died, but I can't tell you how;
He left me six horses to drive in my plow;
With my wing, wang, waddle O, Jack sing saddle O,
Blowsey boys bubble O, under the broom.

I sold my six horses, and bought me a cow;
I'd fain have made a fortune, but did not know how.
With my wing, wang, waddle O, Jack sing saddle O,
Blowsey boys bubble O, under the broom.

I sold my cow, and I bought me a calf;
I'd fain have made a fortune, but lost the best half.
With my wing, wang, waddle O, Jack sing saddle O,
Blowsey boys bubble O, under the broom.

I sold my calf, and bought me a cat;
A pretty thing she was, in my chimney sat,
With my wing, wang, waddle O, Jack sing saddle O,
Blowsey boys bubble O, under the broom.

I sold my cat, and bought me a mouse;
He carried fire in his tail, and burnt down my house;
With my wing, wang, waddle O, Jack sing saddle O,
Blowsey boys bubble O, under the broom.

BOBBY SHAFTOE

Bobby Shaftoe's gone to sea,
    Silver buckles on his knee;
He'll come back and marry me,
    Pretty Bobby Shaftoe.

Bobby Shaftoe's fat and fair,
    Combing down his yellow hair;
He's my love forevermore,
    Pretty Bobby Shaftoe.

Old King Cole was a merry old soul,
And a merry old soul was he;
He called for his pipe, and he called for his bowl,
And he called for his fiddlers three.

Every fiddler, he had a fine fiddle,
And a very fine fiddle had he;
Twee, tweedle-dee, tweedle-dee, went the fiddlers.
Oh, there's none so rare as can compare
With King Cole and his fiddlers three.

Old King Cole was a merry old soul,
And a merry old soul was he;
He called for his pipe, and he called for his bowl,
And he called for his harpers three.

Every harper, he had a fine harp,
And a very fine harp had he.
Twang, twang-a-twang went the harpers,
Twee, tweedle-dee, tweedle-dee went the fiddler
Oh, there's none so rare as can compare
With King Cole and his harpers three!

Oh, Who Is So Merry

Oh, who is so merry, so merry, heigh ho!
As the light-hearted fairy, heigh ho! heigh ho!
  He dances and sings
  To the sound of his wings,
With a hey and a heigh and a ho!

Oh, who is so merry, so airy, heigh ho!
As the light-hearted fairy, heigh ho! heigh ho!
  His nectar he sips
  From a primrose's lips,
With a hey and a heigh and a ho!

Oh, who is so merry, so merry, heigh ho!
As the light-footed fairy, heigh ho! heigh ho!
  His night is the noon
  And his sun is the moon,
With a hey and a heigh and a ho!

COLE

Old King Cole was a merry old soul,
And a merry old soul was he;
He called for his pipe, and he called for his bowl,
And he called for his pipers three.

Every piper he had a fine pipe,
And a very fine pipe had he.
Then tootle, tootle-too, tootle-too went the pipers,
Twang, twang-a-twang, twang-a-twang went the harpers,
Twee, tweedle-dee, tweedle-dee went the fiddlers.
Oh, there's none so rare as can compare
With King Cole and his pipers three!

Old King Cole was a merry old soul,
And a merry old soul was he;
He called for his pipe, and he called for his bowl,
And he called for his drummers three.

Every drummer he had a fine drum,
And a very fine drum had he.
Then rub, rub-a-dub, rub-a-dub
  went the drummers,
Tootle, tootle-too, tootle-too went the pipers,
Twang, twang-a-twang, twang-a-twang
  went the harpers,
Twee, tweedle-dee, tweedle-dee went the fiddlers.
Oh, there's none so rare as can compare
With King Cole and his drummers three!

Ladybird!

Ladybird! Ladybird! fly away home;
Your house is on fire, your children all gone;
All but one, and her name is Ann,
And she crept under the pudding pan.

Ladybird! Ladybird! fly away home;
The field mouse is gone to her nest.
The daisies have shut up their sleepy red eyes,
And the bees and the birds are at rest.

Ladybird! Ladybird! fly away home,
The glowworm is lighting her lamp.
The dew's falling fast, and your fine speckled wings
Will flag with the close-clinging damp.

Ladybird! Ladybird— fly away home;
The fairy bells tinkle afar.
Make haste, or they'll catch you and harness you fast
With a cobweb to Oberon's car.

FA, FE, FI, FO, FUM!

Fa, Fe, Fi, Fo, Fum!
I smell the blood of an Englishman;
Be he alive or be he dead,
I'll grind his bones to make my bread.

My father left me three acres of land

My father left me three acres of land,
  Sing ivy, sing ivy;
My father left me three acres of land,
  Sing holly, go whistle, and ivy !

I plowed it with a ram's horn,
  Sing ivy, sing ivy;
And sowed it all over with one peppercorn,
  Sing holly, go whistle, and ivy!

I harrowed it with a bramble bush,
  Sing ivy, sing ivy;
And reaped it with my little penknife,
  Sing holly, go whistle, and ivy!

I got the mice to carry it to the barn
  Sing ivy, sing ivy;
And thrashed it with a goose's quill,
  Sing holly, go whistle, and ivy!

I got the cat to carry it to the mill,
  Sing ivy, sing ivy;
The miller he swore he would have her paw,
And the cat she swore she would scratch his face,
  Sing holly, go whistle, and ivy!

Doctor Faustus

Doctor Faustus was a good man,
He whipped his scholars now and then;
When he whipped them he made them dance
Out of England into France,
Out of France into Spain,
And then he whipped them back again!

MERRY ARE THE BELLS

Merry are the bells, and merry would they ring,
Merry was myself, and merry could I sing.
With a merry ding-dong, happy, gay and free,
And a merry sing-song, happy let us be!

Waddle goes your gait, and hollow are your hose.
Noddle goes your pate and purple is your nose;
Merry is your sing-song, happy, gay and free,
With a merry ding-dong, happy let us be.

Merry have we met, and merry have we been,
Merry let us part, and merry meet again;
With a merry sing-song, happy, gay and free,
And a merry ding-dong, happy let us be!

I LOVE LITTLE PUSSY

I love little pussy, her coat is so warm,
And if I don't hurt her, she'll do me no harm.
So I'll not pull her tail, nor drive her away,
But pussy and I very gently will play.
I'll sit by the fire, and give her some food,
And pussy will love me because I am good.

SPANISH LAD

Spanish lad, Spanish lad, whence did you come?
From a far-distant, sunny and much-loved home.
I was born, little maid, in the sweet orange grove,
And I wish I was back with the friends that I love.

I THINK SO, DON'T YOU?

If many men knew what many men know,
If many men went where many men go,
If many men did what many men do,
The world would be better; I think so, don't you?

If muffins and crumpets grew already toasted,
And sucking pigs ran about already roasted,
And the bushes were covered with jackets all new,
It would be convenient; I think so, don't you?

Georgie Porgie

Georgie Porgie, pudding and pie,
Kissed the girls and made them cry;
When the boys came out to play,
Georgie Porgie ran away.

LITTLE POLLY FLINDERS

Little Polly Flinders sat among the cinders,
Warming her pretty little toes!
Her mother came and caught her,
And whipped her little daughter,
For spoiling her nice new clothes.

JOHNNY'S TOO LITTLE TO WHITTLE

Johnny's too little to whittle,
Give him some raspberry jam,
Take off his bib, put him into his crib,
And feed him on doughnuts and ham.

LITTLE GIRL, LITTLE GIRL

Little girl, little girl, where have you been?
Gathering roses to give to the Queen.
Little girl, little girl, what gave she you!
She gave me a diamond as big as my shoe.

TOMMY SNOOKS AND BESSY BROOKS

As Tommy Snooks and Bessy Brooks
Were walking out one Sunday.
Says Tommy Snooks to Bessy Brooks,
Tomorrow will be Monday.

HEY DIDDLE DINKETTY

Hey diddle dinketty poppety pet,
The merchants of London they wear scarlet;
Silk in the collar, and gold in the hem,
So merrily march the merchantmen.

THE LITTLE BIRD

Once I saw a little bird
Come hop, hop, hop;
So I cried, "Little bird,
Will you stop, stop, stop?"

And was going to the window
To say, "How do you do?"
But he shook his little tail
And far away he flew.

The Daughter of the Farrier

The daughter of the farrier
Could find no one to marry her,
     Because she said
     She would not wed
A man who could not carry her.

The foolish girl was wrong enough,
And had to wait quite long enough;
     For as she sat
     She grew so fat
That nobody was strong enough!

Terence McDiddler

Terence McDiddler,
The three-stringed fiddler,
Can charm, if he please,
The fish from the seas.

THERE WAS A LITTLE WOMAN

There was a little woman, as I've been told,
Who was not very young, nor yet very old;
Now this little woman her living got
By selling codlins, hot, hot, hot!

HERE'S SULKY SUE

Here's Sulky Sue,
What shall we do?
Turn her face to the wall
Till she comes to.

LITTLE TOMMY TUCKER

Little Tommy Tucker
Sings for his supper.
What shall he eat?
White bread and butter.

How will he cut it
Without e'er a knife?
How can he marry
Without e'er a wife?

I HAD A HOBBY-HORSE

I had a little hobby-horse,
And it was dapple gray,
Its head was made of pea-straw,
Its tail was made of hay.

I sold it to an old woman
For a copper groat;
And I'll not sing my song again
Without another coat.

Sleep, Baby, Sleep

Sleep, baby, sleep,
Our cottage vale is deep:
The little lamb is on the green,
With wooly fleece so soft and clean--
Sleep, baby, sleep.

Sleep, baby, sleep,
Down where the woodbines creep;
Be always like the lamb so mild,
A kind and sweet and gentle child.
Sleep, baby, sleep.

Little Miss Donnet

Little Miss Donnet
Wears a huge bonnet
And hoops half as wide
As the mouth of the Clyde.

ALAS! ALAS!

Alas! alas! for Miss Mackay!
Her knives and forks have run away;
And when the cups and spoons are going,
She's sure there is no way of knowing.

DANCE, THUMBKIN, DANCE

Dance, Thumbkin, dance;
Dance, ye merrymen, everyone.
For Thumbkin, he can dance alone,
Thumbkin, he can dance alone.

Dance, Foreman, dance;
Dance, ye merrymen, everyone.
For Foreman, he can dance alone,
Foreman, he can dance alone.

Dance, Longman, dance;
Dance, ye merrymen, everyone.
For Longman, he can dance alone,
Longman, he can dance alone.

Dance, Ringman, dance;
Dance, ye merrymen, everyone.
But Ringman cannot dance alone,
Ringman cannot dance alone.

Dance, Littleman, dance;
Dance, ye merrymen, everyone.
For Littleman, he can dance alone,
Littleman, he can dance alone.

BAA, BAA, BLACK SHEEP

Baa, baa, black sheep, have you any wool?
Yes, sir, yes, sir, three bags full:
One for my master, one for my dame,
And one for the little boy that lives in our lane.

AS I WAS GOING UP PIPPIN HILL

As I was going up Pippin Hill,
  Pippin Hill was dirty;
There I met a pretty Miss,
  And she dropped me a curtsey.

Little Miss, pretty Miss,
  Blessings light upon you;
If I had half-a-crown a day,
  I'd spend it all upon you.

COCKS CROW

Cocks crow in the morn
　To tell us to rise,
And he who lies late
　Will never be wise.

For early to bed
　And early to rise,
Is the way to be healthy
　And wealthy and wise.

A Swarm of Bees

A swarm of bees in May
Is worth a load of hay;
A swarm of bees in June
Is worth a silver spoon;
A swarm of bees in July
Is not worth a fly.

Butterfly, butterfly,
　Whence do you come?
I know not, I ask not,
　I never had home.

Butterfly, butterfly,
　Where do you go?
Where the sun shines, and
　Where the buds grow.

THERE WAS A CROOKED MAN

There was a crooked man, and he went a crooked mile,
He found a crooked sixpence against a crooked stile;
He bought a crooked cat, which caught a crooked mouse,
And they all lived together in a little crooked house.

81

The Owl and the Eel and the Warming Pan

The owl and the eel and the warming pan,
They went to call on the soap-fat man.
The soap-fat man, he was not within;
He'd gone for a ride on his rolling-pin;
So they all came back by the way of the town,
And turned the meeting-house upside down.

The Man in the Wilderness

The man in the wilderness asked of me
How many strawberries grew in the sea.
I answered him, as I thought good,
"As many as herrings grow in the wood."

When I Was a Little Girl

When I was a little girl, seven years old,
I hadn't got a petticoat to cover from the cold;
So I went into Darlington, that pretty little town,
And there I brought a petticoat, a cloak, and a gown.

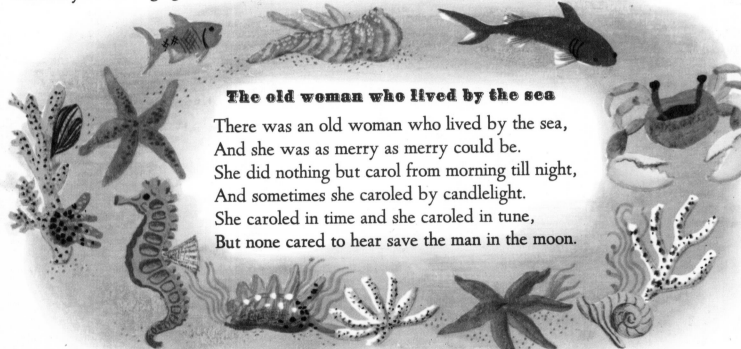

The old woman who lived by the sea

There was an old woman who lived by the sea,
And she was as merry as merry could be.
She did nothing but carol from morning till night,
And sometimes she caroled by candlelight.
She caroled in time and she caroled in tune,
But none cared to hear save the man in the moon.

The Winds

Mister East gave a feast;
Mister North laid the cloth;
Mister West did his best;
Mister South burnt his mouth
Eating cold potato.

I had a cow

I had a little cow,
Hey-diddle, ho-diddle!
I had a little cow,
And it had a little calf,
Hey-diddle, ho-diddle!
And there's my song half.

I had a little cow,
Hey-diddle, ho-diddle!
I had a little cow
And I drove it to the stall,
Hey-diddle, ho-diddle!
And there's my song all!

Leg over Leg

Leg over leg,
As the dog went to Dover;
When he came to a stile
Hop! he went over.

Tom, Tom, the piper's son

Tom, Tom, the piper's son
Stole a pig and away he run.
The pig was eat and Tom was beat,
And Tom went crying down the street.

Tom, Tom, the piper's son,
He learned to play when he was young;
But all the tunes that he could play
Was "Over the hills and far away."

They That Wash on Monday

They that wash on Monday
  Have all the week to dry;
They that wash on Tuesday
  Are not so much awry;
They that wash on Wednesday
  Are not so much to blame;
They that wash on Thursday
  Wash for shame;
They that wash on Friday
  Wash in need;
And they that wash on Saturday,
  Oh, they are slow indeed!

Come to the Window

Come to the window,
My baby, with me,
And look at the stars
That shine on the sea!
There are two little stars
That play at bo-peep
With two little fish
Far down in the deep:
And two little frogs
Cry neap, neap, neap;
I see a dear baby
That should be asleep.

What are little boys made of?

What are little boys made of, made of?
What are little boys made of?
Frogs and snails, and puppy-dogs' tails,
That's what little boys are made of.

What are little girls made of, made of?
What are little girls made of?
Sugar and spice, and all that's nice;
That's what little girls are made of.

Charley Loves Good Cakes

Charley loves good cakes and ale,
Charley loves good candy,
Charley loves to kiss the girls
When they are clean and handy.

Hickety, Pickety

Hickety, pickety, my black hen,
She lays eggs for gentlemen;
Gentlemen come every day
To see what my black hen doth lay.

MOTHER, MAY I GO OUT TO SWIM?

Mother, may I go out to swim?
Yes, my darling daughter.
Hang your clothes on a hickory limb
But don't go near the water.

TO BED, TO BED!

To bed, to bed!'' says Sleepy-head.
''Tarry awhile,'' says Slow.
''Put on the pan,'' says greedy Nan.
''We'll sup before we go.''

DAME GET UP

Dame, get up and bake your pies,
Bake your pies, bake your pies,
Dame, get up and bake your pies
On Christmas day in the morning.

I BOUGHT A DOZEN NEW-LAID EGGS

I bought a dozen new-laid eggs,
Of good old farmer Dickens;
I hobbled home upon two legs,
And found them full of chickens.

DONKEY, DONKEY

Donkey, donkey, old and gray,
Open your mouth and gently bray;
Lift your ears and blow your horn,
To wake the world this sleepy morn.

WASN'T IT FUNNY?

Wasn't it funny? Hear it, all people!
Little Tom Thumb has swallowed a steeple!
How did he do it? I'll tell you, my son!
'Twas made of white sugar, and easily done!

THIS LITTLE PIG

This little pig went to market;
This little pig stayed at home;
This little pig had roast beef;
This little pig had none;
This little pig said, "Wee, wee, wee!"
All the way home.

GREGORY GRIGGS

Gregory Griggs, Gregory Griggs,
Had twenty-seven different wigs.
He wore them up, he wore them down,
To please the people of the town;
He wore them east, he wore them west,
But he never could tell which he liked best.

WEE WILLIE WINKIE

Wee Willie Winkie runs through the town,
Upstairs and downstairs, in his nightgown;
Rapping at the window, crying through the lock,
"Are the children in their beds? Now it's eight o'clock."

LITTLE POLL PARROT

Little Poll Parrot
Sat in a garret,
Eating toast and tea;
A little brown mouse
Jumped into the house
And took it all away.

TWO LITTLE DOGS

Two little dogs
Sat by the fire,
Over a fender of coal-dust;
Said one little dog
To the other little dog,
"If you don't talk, why, I must."

LITTLE TEE WEE

Little Tee Wee,
He went to sea
In an open boat;
And while afloat
The little boat bended,
And my story's ended.

A MAN AND A MAID

There was a little man
Who wooed a little maid,
And he said, "Little maid, will you wed, wed, wed?
 I have little more to say,
 Than will you, yea or nay,
For least said is soonest mended-ded, ded."

Margaret Wrote a Letter

Margaret wrote a letter,
Sealed it with her finger,
Threw it in the dam
For the dusty miller.

Dusty was his coat,
Dusty was the siller,
Dusty was the kiss
I'd from the dusty miller.

If I had my pockets
Full of gold and siller,
I would give it all
To my dusty miller.

WHERE ARE YOU GOING, My Pretty Maid?

"Where are you going, my pretty maid?"
"I'm going a-milking, sir," she said.
"May I go with you, my pretty maid?"
"You're kindly welcome, sir," she said.

"What is your father, my pretty maid?"
"My father's a farmer, sir," she said.
"What is your fortune, my pretty maid?"
"My face is my fortune, sir," she said.

"Then I can't marry you, my pretty maid!"
"Nobody asked you, sir!" she said.

IFS AND ANDS

If "ifs" and "ands"
Were pots and pans,
There'd be no need for tinkers' hands.

THE OLD WOMAN IN THE SHOE

There was an old woman who lived in a shoe.
  She had so many children she didn't know what to do.
She gave them some broth, without any bread,
  And whipped them all soundly, and sent them to bed.

THERE WAS A MAN IN OUR TOWN

There was a man in our town,
And he was wondrous wise;
He jumped into a bramble bush
And scratched out both his eyes.
And when he saw his eyes were out,
With all his might and main
He jumped into another bush
And scratched them in again.

SOLOMON GRUNDY

Solomon Grundy,
Born on Monday,
Christened on Tuesday,
Married on Wednesday,
Took ill on Thursday,
Worse on Friday,
Died on Saturday,
Buried on Sunday.
This is the end
Of Solomon Grundy.

COW, COW

Cow, cow, come blow your horn,
And you shall have a peck of corn.

BIRD, OH, BIRD, COME UNDER MY BONNET

Bird, oh, bird, come under my bonnet,
And you shall have bread with honey upon it;
You shall have sugar in coffee, and tea,
And play every day with baby and me.

87

Peter, Peter

Peter, Peter, pumpkin eater,
Had a wife and couldn't keep her;
He put her in a pumpkin shell,
And there he kept her very well.

The Miller He Grinds

The miller he grinds his corn, his corn;
The miller he grinds his corn, his corn;
The little boy blue comes winding his horn,
With a hop, step, and a jump.

The carter he whistles aside his team,
The carter he whistles aside his team;
And Dolly comes tripping with nice thick cream,
With a hop, step, and a jump.

The nightingale sings when we're at rest,
The nightingale sings when we're at rest;
The little bird climbs the tree for his nest,
With a hop, step, and a jump.

The damsels are churning for curds and whey,
The damsels are churning for curds and whey;
The lads in the field are making the hay,
With a hop, step, and a jump.

JOCKETY, JOG

Jockety jog, jockety jog,
Over the hills and over the bog.

Jockety jog, jockety jog,
Many a mile this day I've trod.

Jockety jog, jockety jog,
I'm the milkman's horse, old Naggetty Nogg.

Jockety jog, jockety jog,
My master's name is Reuney K. Rogg.

THE FAT MAN OF BOMBAY

There was a fat man of Bombay,
Who was smoking one sunshiny day
   When a bird called a snipe
   Flew away with his pipe,
Which vexed the fat man of Bombay.

I Love Sixpence

I love sixpence, pretty little sixpence,
I love sixpence better than my life;
I spent a penny of it, I spent another,
And I took fourpence home to my wife.

Oh, my little fourpence, pretty little fourpence,
I love fourpence better than my life;
I spent a penny of it, I spent another,
And I took twopence home to my wife.

Oh, my little twopence, pretty little twopence,
I love twopence better than my life;
I spent a penny of it, I spent another,
And I took nothing home to my wife.

ockety jog, jockety jog,
'll bear him safe through all this fog.

ockety jog, jockety jog,
'll not stumble over that log.

Jockety jog, jockety jog,
Over the hills and over the bog.

Jockety jog, jockety jog,
Safely home through all the fog.

Jockety jog, jockety jog,
Safely home, Reuney K. Rogg.

Jockety jog, jockety jog,
Safely home, old Naggetty Nogg.

COCK-A-DOODLE-DOO!

Cock-a-doodle-doo!
My dame has lost her shoe;
My master's lost his fiddling-stick,
And don't know what to do.

Cock-a-doodle-doo!
What is my dame to do?
Till master finds his fiddling-stick
She'll dance without her shoe.

Cock-a-doodle-doo!
My dame has lost her shoe;
And master's found his fiddling-stick,
Sing doodle doodle doo!

Cock-a-doodle-doo!
My dame will dance with you,
While master fiddles his fiddling-stick,
For dame and doodle doo.

Cock-a-doodle-doo!
Dame has lost her shoe;
Gone to bed and scratched her head,
And can't tell what to do.

I HAD A LITTLE HUSBAND

I had a little husband, no bigger than my thumb;
I put him in a pint-pot, and there I bid him drum.
I gave him some garters, to garter up his hose,
And a little pocket handkerchief to wipe his pretty nose.

MISTRESS MARY

Mistress Mary, quite contrary,
How does your garden grow?
With cockle shells and silver bells
And pretty maids all in a row.

90

LITTLE DAME CRUMP

Little Dame Crump
With her little hair-broom
Was carefully sweeping
Her little bedroom.
"Hobs-bobs," cried the Dame,
"A penny I spy.
To market I'll go
And a pig I'll buy."

HEIGH-HO, THE CARRION CROW

A carrion crow sat on an oak,
    Fol de riddle, lol de riddle, hi ding do,
Watching a tailor shape his cloak;
    Sing heigh-ho, the carrion crow,
    Fol de riddle, lol de riddle, hi ding do!

Wife! bring me my old bent bow,
    Fol de riddle, lol de riddle, hi ding do,
That I may shoot yon carrion crow;
    Fol de riddle, lol de riddle, hi ding do!

The tailor he shot, and missed his mark,
    Fol de riddle, lol de riddle, hi ding do,
And shot his own sow quite through the heart;
    Sing heigh-ho, the carrion crow,
    Fol de riddle, lol de riddle, hi ding do!

Wife! bring brandy in a spoon,
    Fol de riddle, lol de riddle, hi ding do,
For our old sow is in a swoon;
    Sing heigh-ho, the carrion crow,
    Fol de riddle, lol de riddle, hi ding do!

BYE, BABY BUNTING

Bye, baby bunting,
Daddy's gone a-hunting,
To get a little rabbit's skin
To wrap his baby bunting in.

FOR WANT OF A NAIL

For want of a nail, the shoe was lost;

For want of the shoe, the horse was lost;

For want of the horse, the rider was lost;

For want of the rider, the battle was lost;

For want of the battle, the kingdom was lost,

And all for the want of a horseshoe nail.

OLD MISTRESS MAC

Old Mistress McShuttle
Lived in a coal scuttle,
Along with her dog and her cat:
What they ate I can't tell,
But 'tis known very well
That none of the party was fat.

WE'RE ALL IN THE DUMPS

We're all in the dumps,
For diamonds are trumps,
The kittens are gone to St. Paul's!
The babies are bit,
The moon's in a fit,
And the houses are built without walls.

SIPPITY SUP, SIPPITY SUP

Sippity sup, sippity sup,
Bread and milk from a china cup,
Bread and milk from a bright silver spoon,
Made of a piece of the bright silver moon!
Sippity sup, sippity sup,
Sippity, sippity sup!

AN APPLE PIE

An apple pie, when it looks nice,
Would make one long to have a slice,
But if the taste should prove so, too,
I fear one slice would scarcely do.
So to prevent my asking twice,
Pray, Mamma, cut a good large slice.

OH, RARE HARRY PARRY

Oh, rare Harry Parry,
    When will you marry?
When apples and peaches are ripe.
    I'll come to your wedding,
    Without any bidding,
And dance and sing all the night.

Oh, dear, what can the matter be!

Oh, dear, what can the matter be?
Oh, dear, what can the matter be?
Oh, dear, what can the matter be?
    Johnny's so long at the Fair!

He promised he'd buy me a bunch of blue ribbons,
He promised he'd buy me a bunch of blue ribbons,
He promised he'd buy me a bunch of blue ribbons,
    To tie up my bonny brown hair.

OH, DEAR! WHAT CAN THE MATTER BE?

Oh, dear! what can the matter be?
Two old women got up in an apple tree;
One came down, and the other stayed till Saturday.

BOW, WOW, WOW!

Bow, wow, wow!
    Whose dog art thou?
Little Tommy Tinker's dog,
    Bow, wow, wow!

A GOOD CHILD

A good child, a good child,
As I suppose you be,
Will never laugh nor smile
At the tickling of your knee.

HICKUP, HICKUP

Hickup, hickup, go away!
Come again another day;
Hickup, hickup, when I bake,
I'll give you a butter cake.

AT EARLY MORN THE SPIDERS SPIN

At early morn the spiders spin,
And by and by the flies drop in;
And when they call, the spiders say,
"Take off your things and stay all day.
Where have you been all the day?"

The Little Girl with the Curl

There was a little girl, who had a little curl
Right in the middle of her forehead;
When she was good she was very, very good
But when she was bad she was horrid.

Hector Protector

Hector Protector was dressed all in green;
Hector Protector was sent to the Queen.
The Queen did not like him, no more did the King,
So Hector Protector was sent back again.

PETER PIPER

Peter Piper picked a peck of pickled peppers;
A peck of pickled peppers Peter Piper picked.
If Peter Piper picked a peck of pickled peppers,
Where's the peck of pickled peppers Peter Piper picked?

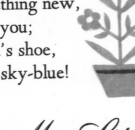

Oh, listen my doll

Oh, listen, my doll, and hear something new,
You're not to repeat, 'tis only for you;
Mark! pussy has stolen grandpapa's shoe,
And Topsy has painted dog Fido sky-blue!

Little maid, pretty maid

"Little maid, pretty maid, whither goest thou?"
"Down in the forest to milk my cow."
"Shall I go with thee?" "No, not now;
When I send for thee, then come thou."

My Little Hen

I had a little hen, the prettiest ever seen,
She washed me the dishes and kept the house clean;
She went to the mill to fetch me some flour;
She brought it home in less than an hour;
She baked me my bread, she brewed me my ale;
She sat by the fire and told many a fine tale.

Little Nobby Colt

There was a little nobby colt,
   His name was Nobby Gray;
His head was made of pouce straw,
   His tail was made of hay.

Ply the Spade

Ply the spade
And ply the hoe,
Plant the seed
And it will grow.

When I Was a Little Boy

When I was a little boy,
I washed my mother's floor;
Now I am a man of wealth,
And drive a coach and four.

Sing, sing

Sing, sing, what shall I sing?
The cat's run away with the pudding-string!
Do, do, what shall I do?
The cat has bitten it quite in two.

If I had a little mule, sir

If I had a mule, sir, and he wouldn't start,
Do you think I'd harness him up to a cart?
No, no, I'd give him oats and hay,
And let him stay there all the day.

As I Was Going to Market

As I was going to market upon a market day,
I met the finest ram, sir, that ever fed on hay,
  On hay, on hay, on hay--
I met the finest ram, sir, that ever fed on hay.

This ram was fat behind, sir; this ram was fat before;
This ram was ten yards round, sir; indeed he was no more,
  No more, no more, no more--
This ram was ten yards round, sir; indeed he was no more.

The horns grew on his head, sir, they were so wondrous high,
As I've been plainly told, sir, they reached up to the sky,
  The sky, the sky, the sky--
As I've been plainly told, sir, they reached up to the sky.

The tail grew on his back, sir, was six yards and an ell,
And it was sent to market to toll the market bell,
  The bell, the bell, the bell--
And it was sent to market to toll the market bell.

There was an old woman who rode on a broom

There was an old woman who rode on a broom,
With a high gee ho, gee humble;
And she took her old cat behind for a groom,
With a bimble, bamble, bumble.

Rock-a-bye, baby, thy cradle is green

Rock-a-bye, baby, thy cradle is green;
Father's a nobleman, mother's a queen;
And Betty's a lady, and wears a gold ring;
And Johnny's a drummer, and drums for the King.

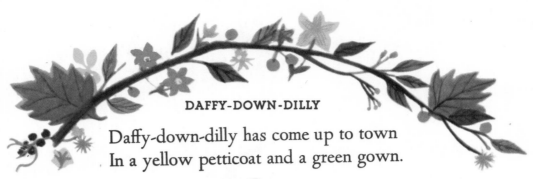

DAFFY-DOWN-DILLY

Daffy-down-dilly has come up to town
In a yellow petticoat and a green gown.

THE LITTLE MAID

There was a little maid
And she had a light guitar,
And when the moon was bright,
She sang tra, la, tra, la.

PIPING HOT

Piping hot, smoking hot,
  What I've got
  You have not.
Hot gray pease, hot, hot, hot;
Hot gray pease, hot.

TWO BLACKBIRDS

There were two blackbirds,
Sitting on a hill,
The one named Jack,
  The other named Jill;
Fly away, Jack! Fly away, Jill!
Come again, Jack! Come again, Jill!

YOU SHALL HAVE AN APPLE

You shall have an apple,
You shall have a plum,
You shall have a rattle
When your dad comes home.

I SING, I SING

I sing, I sing,
From morn till night,
From cares I'm free,
And my heart is light.